THE STAR WARS™ COOKBOOK

BB-ATE | AWAKEN TO THE FORCE OF BREAKFAST AND BRUNCH

BY LARA STARR / PHOTOGRAPHY BY MATTHEW CARDEN

CHRONICLE BOOKS
SAN FRANCISCO

www.starwars.com

Library of Congress Cataloging-in-Publication Data available.

ISBN 978-1-4521-6298-0

Manufactured by Midas Printing, Huizhou, Guangdong, China, in August 2017.

Figures and vehicles courtesy of Hasbro.

Art direction and concepts by Matthew Carden.
Styling by Jennifer Carden.

10 9 8 7 6 5 4 3 2 1

Chronicle Books
680 Second Street
San Francisco, California 94107
www.chroniclebooks.com

Distributed in Europe by
Abrams & Chronicle Books Limited
161 Farringdon Road, 3rd Floor
London EC1R 3AL

TABLE OF CONTENTS

INTRODUCTION   4

SNACKS & SIDES

BB-8 Energy Balls   8
Kylo's Ren-egade Fruit Bowls   11
Finn's Blazing Fruit Blasters   12
Frozen Yogurt Lightsabers   13
Phasmatic Potato Packets   15
Chewie's Bacon   16

CEREAL

Rose's Galaxy Granola Bars   19
Parfait de Resistance   20
Han Soloatmeal   21

EGGS

Snoke'in Supreme Scramble   23
Rebel Pepper Egg Cups   24
Luggabeast of a Quiche   26
Maz Kanata Frittata   28
Stormtrooper Standoff   31

WAFFLES, PANCAKES & FRENCH TOAST

Luke Skywaffles   33
C-3POat Pancakes   36
Starkiller Pancakes   38
First Order French Toast   41

BAKED GOODS

Admiral Ackbars   43
Canto "Bites"   44
Reysin Bread   46
Pretz-wing Fighters   49

SANDWICHES & WRAPS

Breakfast Poe'Boy   51
Kanjiklub Sandwiches   53
Breakfast Tako-danas   54

SPREADS & TOPPINGS

A Tight Jam   58
"Light It Up" Lemon Curd   60

DRINKS

Vitamin C-3PO   63
Jakku Juice   64

INTRODUCTION

The Force is strong in your kitchen. Your oven has it. Your freezer has it. This book has it. You have that power, too. With these recipes, the breakfasts and brunches you seek will be brimming with intergalactic goodness.

Some of these recipes are simple enough to make on your own and enjoy with family and friends. Others require the help of an adult. Be sure to get your parents or other grown-ups involved. Seek the wisdom of their cooking experience.

As you prepare yourself for the day ahead, you will want the aid of this cookbook and the light of the Force to help guide your way. Adventure and tastiness will be yours as you blast your way to a better breakfast and fulfill your delicious destiny. Like Rey, you may even discover hidden abilities that you didn't know you had. Accept the challenge, young Padawan, and feel the Force!

GETTING STARTED

Before you start making these recipes, you must master some essential safety steps. The kitchen is a place of peace, yet danger lurks in the most ordinary places. The two most important rules to remember are:

1. Keep an adult in the kitchen at all times, especially when you use knives, the stovetop, or the oven. Adults make good company and are helpful and handy to have around. (Even Rey and Finn would have been toast without Han to guide and protect them.) Remember, never use anything sharp or hot without an adult to guide you.

2. Wash your hands with soap and warm water before cooking. Remember the hideous creatures in Maz Kanata's tavern on Takodana? They are nothing compared to what may reside on your hands. Fight those microscopic life-forms with your best weapons: soap and water. It's a good idea to wash your hands a few times while you're cooking too; like Kylo Ren and the First Order, the germ troops are known to send in constant reinforcements.

The calm and perceptive mind of a Jedi warrior will enable you to prevent most mishaps in the kitchen. Use it well and follow these general guidelines.

BE CAREFUL

Respect the mysteries of the Force.

> Never run in the kitchen.

> Keep everything—pot holders, towels, packages of ingredients, this book— away from burners on the stove. The stove can be hot even if the burners are all turned off.

> Dry your hands before turning on any electric switch or putting in or pulling out a plug.

> Wash knives and other sharp utensils one at a time. Don't drop them in a pan or bucket of soapy water—you may cut yourself when you reach in to fish them out.

> Lift lids on hot pots at an angle away from you, directing the rising steam away from your face.

> Use only dry pot holders and oven mitts. Wet ones will give you a steam burn when you touch the handle of a hot pot.

> Put a pot or pan on the stove before you turn on the heat.

> Turn off the heat before you remove a pot or pan from the stove.

> Never put out a grease fire with water. Water causes grease to splatter and can spread the fire very quickly. To put out a grease fire, smother it with a tight-fitting lid or throw handfuls of baking soda onto it.

BE AWARE

Cultivate the awareness of a Jedi.

> Never leave the kitchen while something is cooking on the stove or in the oven.

> Keep pot handles away from the edge of the stove so no one passing by topples the pot.

> Always position pot handles away from other stove burners. Otherwise, they'll get hot and burn you when you go to move the pot.

> Remove utensils from hot pots when you're not using them, placing them on a plate or spoon holder near the stove. Metal spoons and spatulas are especially dangerous, because they'll absorb and hold the heat and burn your hand when you go to use them.

> Start with a clean kitchen and keep it clean as you cook. When something spills, wipe it up immediately to keep accidents from happening. If you have time, wash dishes as you go.

> Turn off the blender's motor before removing the lid.

> Put ingredients away when you're finished with them.

> Know where to find the fire extinguisher and be sure it's in working order.

The tools of a Jedi chef are powerful but simple. You probably already have everything in your kitchen. Here's an alphabetical list of what you may need.

EQUIPMENT

Aluminum foil

Baking dishes

Baking sheets

Black permanent marker

Blender*

Cheese grater

Colander

Electric mixer*

Fine-mesh strainer

Fire extinguisher

Food coloring

Food processor

Ice cube tray

Knives* (one large and one small)

Ladle

Lidded pint jar

Measuring cups and spoons

Mixing bowls of various sizes

Muffin pan (12 cups)

Nonstick cooking spray

Oven mitts

Parchment paper

Pastry brush

Plastic cups

Plastic wrap

Pot holders

Rubber and metal spatulas

Saucepans with lids

Skillet

Squeeze bottle

Tall glasses

Tea towel

Toaster oven*

Tongs*

Wax paper

Whisk

Wire rack

Wooden skewers*

Wooden spoons

*Use these items with extreme caution. Definitely get an adult to assist you whenever you need to use them.

Go forth, young Jedi! May your newfound abilities free you from hunger, and may the Force always be with you!

SNACKS
& SIDES

BB-8 Energy Balls

Kylo's Ren-egade Fruit Bowls

Finn's Blazing Fruit Blasters

Frozen Yogurt Lightsabers

Phasmatic Potato Packets

Chewie's Bacon

BB-8 ENERGY BALLS

Sometimes the answer you seek lies within. These energy balls will fuel all of your day's adventures!

INGREDIENTS

1	cup (100 grams) old-fashioned rolled oats
½	cup (130 grams) peanut butter, smooth or crunchy
1	cup (65 grams) chopped dates
2	teaspoons grated orange zest
2	tablespoons fresh orange juice
⅓	cup (115 grams) honey
1	cup (80 grams) unsweetened shredded coconut

1. Put the oats, peanut butter, dates, orange zest, orange juice, and honey in the bowl of a food processor or blender. Pulse on medium speed until the ingredients are well combined and form a sticky paste.

2. Scoop out the mixture and place it on a lightly floured surface. Roll the mixture into 1-inch (2.5-centimetre) balls.

3. Put the shredded coconut on a plate or in a shallow bowl. Roll each of the balls in the coconut to cover completely.

4. Serve immediately or store covered in the refrigerator for up to 1 week.

Variation: Roll the balls in ¾ cup (60 grams) unsweetened cocoa powder, or 1 cup (120 grams) finely chopped nuts.

Makes about 25 balls.

KYLO'S REN-EGADE FRUIT BOWLS

INGREDIENTS

6	sheets phyllo dough, thawed according to package directions
½	cup (110 grams) butter, melted
2	cups (240 grams) fresh strawberries, hulled and quartered
2	cups (320 grams) green and/or red grapes, halved

1. Preheat the oven to 400°F (200°C).

2. Coat a 12-cup muffin pan with nonstick cooking spray.

3. Cover the phyllo dough sheets with a damp tea towel. Remove one sheet from the stack and lay it on a flat surface. Using a pastry brush, brush the top of the sheet with some of the melted butter. Place another sheet of phyllo dough on top and continue layering the melted butter and phyllo until all 6 sheets are used, brushing each top sheet with butter as you stack them.

4. Using a knife, cut the stacked phyllo sheets into twelve 4-inch (10-centimetre) squares.

5. Place each square into the cups of the muffin pan, pressing the dough into the sides and letting the corners extend slightly above the tops.

6. Bake until lightly browned and crisp, 10 to 12 minutes. Carefully transfer the muffin pan to a wire rack to cool.

7. Just before serving, combine the strawberries and grapes in a bowl and spoon the mixed fruit into each of the phyllo cups. Serve immediately.

Makes 12 servings.

FINN'S BLAZING FRUIT BLASTERS

Blaze your way into breakfast armed with fresh fruit.

INGREDIENTS

3	large bananas

Assorted fruit, cut into ¾-inch (2-centimetre) pieces:

¼	cup (30 grams) apples
¼	cup (40 grams) grapes
¼	cup (30 grams) fresh strawberries, hulled
¼	cup (35 grams) fresh blueberries
¼	cup (35 grams) pineapple chunks
¼	cup (40 grams) cantaloupe or melon of choice

Special equipment: Five 10-inch (25-centimetre) wooden skewers

1. Line a baking sheet with parchment or wax paper.

2. Cut a 3-inch (7.5-centimetre) segment from each banana. Discard—or eat—the rest of the banana. Thread each banana crosswise onto a 10-inch (25-centimetre) wooden skewer, sliding it about two-thirds of the way down the skewer. Fill the rest of the skewer on either side with the remaining fruit pieces.

3. Break another skewer in half and push it into the bottom of the banana to make the handle of the blaster. Fill the rest of the smaller skewer with fruit. Place the filled skewer on the prepared baking sheet.

4. Repeat with the remaining fruit and skewers. Freeze for at least 1 hour before serving, or cover with plastic wrap and freeze for up to 1 week.

Makes 3 servings.

FROZEN YOGURT LIGHTSABERS

INGREDIENTS

2   **cups (480 grams) low-fat vanilla Greek yogurt**

     Red and blue food coloring

1. The night before serving, set a fine-mesh strainer over a medium bowl. With a rubber spatula, scoop the yogurt into the strainer and let drain in the refrigerator overnight.

2. Discard the drained liquid in the bottom of the bowl. Divide the yogurt into two bowls and color one with red and one with blue food coloring, using 3 or 4 drops of each coloring.

3. Place a large piece of plastic wrap on a flat surface. Spoon half of the red yogurt onto the center of the plastic, spreading it out into a 10-x-1-inch (25-x-2.5-centimetre) rectangle.

4. Fold the plastic wrap over the yogurt and carefully manipulate to shape the yogurt to form a log in the plastic wrap. Twist the ends of the plastic wrap to make a tight, compact shape. Repeat with the remaining yogurt to create 4 logs total (2 red and 2 blue).

5. Place on a baking sheet and freeze overnight.

6. Once frozen, unwrap and eat, or store in the freezer for up to 1 month.

Makes 4 servings.

PHASMATIC POTATO PACKETS

Captain Phasma has shiny metal armor. These savory breakfast potatoes are cooked in shiny aluminum foil pouches.

INGREDIENTS

6	**Russet potatoes, scrubbed and diced**
3	**teaspoons dried rosemary**
1	**large yellow onion, diced**
6	**tablespoons (90 grams) butter**
	Salt and pepper for seasoning
	Garlic powder for sprinkling

1. Preheat the oven to 375°F (190°C).

2. Tear off six 12-inch (30.5-centimetre) squares of aluminum foil. In the center of each square, place one-sixth of the potatoes, ½ teaspoon of the rosemary, one-sixth of the onion, and 1 tablespoon of the butter. Sprinkle each serving with salt, pepper, and garlic powder.

3. Bring up the sides of the foil and fold over to make six packets.

4. Carefully place the folded packets on a baking sheet. Bake for 45 minutes.

5. Cool for approximately 10 minutes before serving. Place each packet on a plate. Serve warm.

Makes 6 servings.

CHEWIE'S BACON

Chewbacca has been by Han Solo's side through many years and adventures. This sweet, chewy bacon is a go-to side for pancakes, waffles, or cereal.

INGREDIENTS

8	bacon slices
1/3	cup (65 grams) packed dark brown sugar

1. Preheat the oven to 400°F (200°C).

2. Line a baking sheet with aluminum foil. Place a wire rack on top of the foil-lined baking sheet and coat with nonstick cooking spray.

3. Put the sugar on a plate. Press both sides of each bacon slice into the sugar.

4. Lay the bacon slices on the wire rack and twist each end several times.

5. Bake until crisp and glazed, 15 to 18 minutes.

6. Cool on the rack for 5 minutes before serving.

Makes 4 servings.

CEREAL

Rose's Galaxy Granola Bars ....

Parfait de Resistance ....

Han Soloatmeal ....

ROSE'S GALAXY GRANOLA BARS

Rose is a mechanic for the Resistance. Refuel with these granola bars.

INGREDIENTS

3	cups (300 grams) old-fashioned rolled oats
1	cup (60 grams) chopped walnuts
½	teaspoon ground cinnamon
½	teaspoon ground ginger
⅔	cup (230 grams) honey
¼	cup (50 grams) packed dark brown sugar
1	teaspoon vanilla extract
¼	teaspoon salt for seasoning
1	cup (160 grams) diced dried apricots

1. Preheat the oven to 350°F (175°C).

2. Combine the oats and walnuts on a baking sheet and toast for 10 minutes, until lightly browned and fragrant, stirring a few times during baking. Transfer to a large mixing bowl, then add the cinnamon and ginger and stir to combine.

3. Lower the oven temperature to 300°F (150°C).

4. In a small saucepan over medium heat, combine the butter, honey, brown sugar, vanilla, and salt and bring to a boil, stirring occasionally until the sugar is dissolved. Carefully pour over the toasted oatmeal mixture. Add the apricots and stir to combine. Let cool for at least 5 minutes.

5. Butter an 8-by-12-inch (20-by-30.5-centimetre) baking dish. Pour the mixture into the prepared baking dish. With wet fingers, gently press the mixture evenly into the dish.

6. Bake for 25 to 30 minutes or until golden. Let cool completely before cutting into bars. Store in an airtight container for up to a week.

Makes 16 bars.

PARFAIT DE RESISTANCE

Rey uses the Force to trick the stormtrooper guards, allowing her to escape custody on Starkiller Base. Make your own escape from hunger with this powerful parfait!

INGREDIENTS

3	cups (720 grams) low-fat vanilla Greek yogurt
1½	cups (180 grams) granola
1	large banana, sliced crosswise

Special equipment: Six 9-fluid-ounce (270-millilitre) clear plastic cups

1. Spoon ⅓ cup (80 grams) yogurt into each 9-ounce (270-millilitre) plastic cups. Using the back of a spoon, spread the yogurt up the sides of the cup, coating the inside evenly.

2. Fill the cup with 2 tablespoons granola, a few banana slices, and another 2 tablespoons granola. Cover the granola with 2 to 3 tablespoons of yogurt, smoothing the top with the back of a spoon. Serve immediately.

Makes 6 servings.

HAN SOLOATMEAL

Han Solo waits a long time before being reunited with General Leia. These overnight oatmeal cups will wait for you in the fridge until you're ready for breakfast.

INGREDIENTS

2	cups (200 grams) old-fashioned rolled oats
2	cups (480 grams) low-fat vanilla yogurt
½	teaspoon ground cinnamon
½	cup (60 grams) chopped walnuts
1	cup (140 grams) fresh blueberries

Special equipment: 4 mason jars

1. In a large bowl, stir together the oats, yogurt, and cinnamon.
2. Divide the oat mixture evenly among the 4 jars.
3. Top the oat mixture with the walnuts and blueberries.
4. Cover the jars and refrigerate overnight.
5. Eat from the jar the next day, or store in the refrigerator for up to 1 week.

Makes 4 servings.

EGGS

Snoke'in Supreme Scramble

Rebel Pepper Egg Cups

Luggabeast of a Quiche

Maz Kanata Frittata

Stormtrooper Standoff

SNOKE'IN SUPREME SCRAMBLE

INGREDIENTS

2	**teaspoons butter**
¼	**cup (35 grams) finely chopped onion**
2	**cups (40 grams) stemmed and washed spinach leaves**
4	**eggs**
¼	**cup (35 grams) sliced black olives**
2	**tablespoons crumbled low-fat feta cheese**

1. In a medium skillet over medium heat, melt the butter. Add the onion and cook, stirring frequently, until translucent, 2 to 3 minutes.

2. Add the spinach and cook, stirring frequently until wilted, 2 to 3 minutes.

3. Using tongs, transfer the vegetables to a plate and set aside.

4. Return the skillet to medium heat. Crack the eggs into a small bowl and whisk with a fork to combine. Pour the eggs into the skillet. When the edges start to set, use a wooden spoon or spatula to gently push the eggs to the center, and tilt the skillet to distribute the uncooked eggs. Swirl the eggs to distribute the uncooked eggs to the surface of the skillet. Continue scraping until the eggs are just cooked through, about 2 minutes. They will be fluffy and appear just a little wet, but not liquidy.

5. Add the cooked vegetables and olives and cook, stirring continuously, until the mixture is completely heated through, 1 to 2 minutes.

6. Divide the scramble between 2 plates and top with the feta cheese. Serve immediately.

Makes 2 servings.

REBEL PEPPER EGG CUPS

Bright red bell peppers, like the red insignia of the Resistance, are a delicious and edible "bowl" for a savory filling of eggs, bacon, and ripe red tomatoes.

INGREDIENTS

3	large red bell peppers, halved lengthwise, seeded, and deribbed
	Salt and pepper for seasoning
6	eggs
1	large tomato, diced
1	cup (80 grams) shredded low-fat Monterey Jack cheese
6	bacon slices, cooked and chopped

1. Preheat the oven to 350°F (180°C).

2. Place the red bell pepper halves on an ungreased baking sheet. Sprinkle with salt and pepper. Bake until soft, 15 to 20 minutes.

3. Meanwhile, whisk the eggs in a large bowl. Add the tomato, cheese, and bacon and stir to combine.

4. Using a ladle or large spoon, distribute the egg mixture evenly into the half-baked peppers. Sprinkle with salt and pepper. Bake for 15 to 20 minutes more, until the eggs are set.

5. Let cool for 10 minutes before serving. Serve warm.

Makes 6 servings.

LUGGABEAST OF A QUICHE

Teedo rides a luggabeast as he scavenges around Jakku. This quiche is made with sausage and cheese, or anything you scavenge from the fridge.

INGREDIENTS

2	tablespoons dried bread crumbs
2	large sweet sausage links, sliced into ¼-inch (6-millimetre) rounds
½	cup (70 grams) chopped onion
8	ounces (230 grams) white or brown mushrooms, sliced
4	eggs
1	cup (240 millilitres) low-fat milk
2	cups (160 grams) shredded low-fat sharp cheddar cheese
½	teaspoon garlic powder
	Salt and pepper for seasoning

1. Preheat the oven to 350°F (180°C).

2. Butter a 9-inch (23-centimetre) glass pie dish. Place the bread crumbs in the dish and swirl and tip to coat. Tap out the excess bread crumbs.

3. Heat a skillet over medium heat. Add the sausage and cook, turning with a spatula a few times, until cooked through, 3 to 4 minutes. Transfer the sausage to a plate and set aside. Add the onions to the skillet and cook, stirring frequently, until translucent, 2 to 3 minutes. Add the mushrooms and cook until soft, 5 to 6 minutes.

4. In a large bowl, whisk together the eggs and milk. Add the cheese, sausage, cooked vegetables, and garlic powder. Season with salt and pepper. Pour the egg mixture into the prepared pie dish.

5. Bake for 30 minutes, until the quiche is set.

6. Remove from the oven and let cool for 15 minutes. To serve, cut the quiche into 6 wedges and remove from the pie dish with a pie server.

Makes 6 servings.

MAZ KANATA FRITTATA

Everyone is welcome at Maz's castle on Takodana. You're welcome to multiple slices of this colorful frittata!

INGREDIENTS

1	tablespoon olive oil
1	small yellow onion, diced
2	large zucchini (about 1 pound/455 grams), sliced into ¼-inch (6-millimetre) rounds
	Salt and pepper for seasoning
8	eggs
¼	cup (20 grams) shredded low-fat mozzarella cheese
¼	cup (60 millimetres) low-fat milk or heavy cream
2	medium tomatoes, cored, halved lengthwise, and sliced

1. Preheat the oven to 400°F (200°C).

2. Heat the olive oil in a medium ovenproof skillet over medium heat. Add the onion and zucchini and season with salt and pepper. Sauté until tender, 8 to 10 minutes. Remove from the heat and set aside.

3. In a large bowl, whisk together the eggs, cheese, and milk. Season with salt and pepper.

4. Pour the egg mixture over the onion and zucchini in the skillet. Gently stir to evenly distribute the eggs and vegetables.

5. Using tongs, place the tomato slices on top of the mixture.

6. Return the skillet to medium heat and cook until the edges begin to set and turn from translucent to opaque, about 1 minute. Transfer the skillet to the oven and bake until the eggs are set and don't jiggle when the pan is moved, 15 to 20 minutes.

7. Cool on a wire rack for 10 minutes before serving warm, or serve at room temperature. To serve, cut into 8 wedges and remove from the skillet with a pie server.

Makes 8 servings.

STORMTROOPER STANDOFF

Face a squadron of stormtrooper hard-boiled eggs before you face the day!

INGREDIENTS

12   eggs

Special equipment: Black permanent marker

1. Place the eggs in a pot large enough for them to all fit on the bottom in a single layer. Add enough cold water to cover the eggs by 1 inch (2.5 centimetres).

2. Bring to a boil over high heat. When just boiling, turn off the heat and cover the pot. Let the eggs stand for 12 minutes.

3. Remove the eggs from the pot with a slotted spoon, transfer to a colander, and rinse under cold water, or place in a bowl of ice water to cool.

4. Once cool, use the illustration on this page as a reference to draw a stormtrooper face on each egg with a black permanent marker.

5. Serve immediately or store in an egg holder in the refrigerator for up to 1 week.

Makes 12 servings.

WAFFLES, PANCAKES & FRENCH TOAST

Luke Skywaffles

C-3POat Pancakes

Starkiller Pancakes

First Order French Toast

LUKE SKYWAFFLES

A cloaked Luke Skywalker stands alone atop a mountain as Rey approaches. The batter for these waffles needs to stand overnight, and when morning approaches you'll wake up to a delectable breakfast.

INGREDIENTS

One	**¼-ounce (7 grams) package or 2½ teaspoons active dry yeast**
¾	**cup (180 millilitres) warm water, 105°F–110°F (40°C–43°C)**
2	**cups (280 grams) all-purpose flour**
1	**cup (160 grams) yellow cornmeal**
2	**tablespoons light brown sugar**
1	**teaspoon salt for seasoning**
2	**cups (480 millilitres) low-fat milk**
¼	**cup (60 millilitres) vegetable oil**
1	**teaspoon vanilla extract**
2	**eggs**
½	**teaspoon baking soda**
	Butter for serving
	Maple syrup for serving

1. The night before serving the waffles, make the batter: In a small bowl, sprinkle the yeast over the warm water and set aside until bubbly, about 10 minutes.

2. Meanwhile, stir together the flour, cornmeal, sugar, and salt in a large bowl.

3. In a separate large bowl, whisk together the milk, vegetable oil, and vanilla. Add the yeast mixture to the milk mixture and continue to whisk until well combined.

Continued

4. Make a well in the flour mixture, then pour in the milk mixture, whisking gently until well combined. Cover the bowl with plastic wrap and refrigerate overnight.

5. The next day, make the waffles: Preheat the waffle iron. In a small bowl, beat or whisk the eggs with the baking soda, then add the mixture to the batter and continue whisking gently until combined.

6. Preheat the oven to 200°F (95°C).

7. Cook the waffles in the waffle iron according to manufacturer's directions. Keep warm in the oven as you make the waffles. Serve warm with butter and maple syrup.

Makes approximately 8 waffles.

C-3POAT PANCAKES

INGREDIENTS

2	cups (200 grams) quick-cooking oats
2	cups (480 millilitres) low-fat milk or buttermilk
2	eggs
¼	cup (60 millilitres) vegetable oil
¾	cup (105 grams) whole-wheat flour
2	tablespoons sugar
1	teaspoon ground cinnamon
2½	teaspoons baking powder
1	teaspoon salt for seasoning
⅓	cup (45 grams) golden raisins
1	teaspoon butter
	Maple syrup for serving
	Jam for serving

1. In a large bowl, soak the oats in the milk for 10 minutes. Add the eggs and oil, whisking to combine.

2. In a separate large bowl, whisk together the flour, sugar, cinnamon, baking powder, and salt. Add the raisins and toss to coat.

3. Add the oat mixture to the flour mixture and stir until just combined.

4. Preheat oven to 200°F (95°C).

5. Heat a skillet over medium heat, add the butter, and swirl until it melts and coats the skillet. Pour ¼ cup (60 millilitres) of batter into the skillet for each pancake. Cook until bubbles appear on the batter's surface, 2 to 3 minutes. Flip with a spatula and cook until golden, 1 to 2 minutes more.

6. Keep the pancakes warm on a baking sheet in the oven. Repeat with the remaining batter.

7. Serve with maple syrup or jam.

Makes 6 servings.

STARKILLER PANCAKES

The Resistance destroys the Starkiller Base with their X-wings. You'll destroy a stack of these cocoa-flavored pancakes with your hunger and a fork!

INGREDIENTS

1	cup (140 grams) all-purpose flour
2	tablespoons sugar
3	tablespoons unsweetened cocoa powder
1	teaspoon baking powder
1	teaspoon salt for seasoning
1	cup plus 1 tablespoon (255 millilitres) low-fat milk
1	egg
1	teaspoon vanilla extract
4	maraschino cherries
	Maple syrup for serving
	Jam for serving

Special equipment: Squeeze bottle

1. Preheat the oven to 200°F (95°C).

2. In a large bowl, whisk together the flour, sugar, 2 tablespoons of the cocoa powder, baking powder, and salt.

3. In a medium bowl, whisk together one cup of the milk, the egg, and vanilla.

4. Make a well in the flour mixture, then pour in the milk mixture, whisking gently until well combined.

5. Using a large spoon and a measuring cup, scoop out ⅓ cup (80 millilitres) of the batter and place it in a small bowl. Add the remaining 1 tablespoon of the cocoa powder and the remaining 1 tablespoon of the milk, then whisk with a fork to combine. Carefully pour into a squeeze bottle.

6. Spray a 12-inch (30.5-centimetre) nonstick skillet with nonstick cooking spray and place over medium heat.

7. Using the bottle as a pen, "draw" a circle with an 8-inch (20-centimetre) diameter onto the heated skillet. Then draw two lines to make a "band" across the center of the circle.

8. Cut each maraschino cherry crosswise into three sections. Discard—or eat—the top and bottom thirds.

9. Using small tongs or a fork, place a cherry crosscut to the left of the band.

10. Using a large spoon or small ladle, fill in the pancake with batter. Cook until bubbles form on the batter's surface, 2 to 3 minutes. Flip the pancake with a spatula and cook for 1 to 2 minutes more, until the bottom is lightly browned.

11. Keep the pancakes warm on a baking sheet in the oven. Repeat steps 7–10 with the remaining batter.

12. Serve with maple syrup or jam.

Makes 4 pancakes.

FIRST ORDER FRENCH TOAST

INGREDIENTS

1	loaf French, sourdough, or whole wheat bread, approximately 1 pound (455 grams), cut into 1-inch (2.5-centimetre) slices
8	eggs
3	cups (720 millilitres) low-fat milk
2	tablespoons sugar
1	teaspoon vanilla extract
2	teaspoons ground cinnamon
	Butter for serving
	Maple syrup for serving

1. Generously butter a 9-x-13-inch (23-x-33-centimetre) baking dish. Arrange the bread slices in the dish, overlapping slightly.

2. In a large bowl, whisk together the eggs, milk, 1 tablespoon of the sugar, and vanilla.

3. Pour the egg mixture evenly over the bread slices. Cover the baking dish with plastic wrap and refrigerate for at least 2 hours or overnight.

4. Preheat the oven to 350°F (180°C).

5. Sprinkle the remaining 1 tablespoon sugar and the cinnamon over the bread slices. Bake until lightly browned and the egg mixture is set, 30 to 40 minutes.

6. Let cool 10 minutes before serving with butter and maple syrup.

Makes 8 servings.

BAKED GOODS

Admiral Ackbars

Canto "Bites"

Reysin Bread

Pretz-wing Fighters

ADMIRAL ACKBARS

It is not a trap! These bars are irresistible!

INGREDIENTS

2	cups (200 grams) quick-cooking oats
1	cup chunky (260 grams) peanut butter
½	cup (60 grams) chopped pecans
½	cup (55 grams) chopped dried apricots
1	teaspoon ground cinnamon
¼	cup (85 grams) honey

1. Prepare an 8-inch (20-centimetre) square baking pan by cutting two 8-x-12-inch (20-x-30.5-centimetre) pieces of parchment paper or wax paper. Crisscross the pieces over the bottom of the pan and press them up against the sides of the pan, allowing the paper to overhang slightly.

2. In a large bowl, stir together the oats, peanut butter, pecans, apricots, cinnamon, and honey until well combined.

3. Press the mixture into the prepared pan, then cover with plastic wrap, pressing it onto the surface of the mixture, and refrigerate for at least 3 hours or overnight.

4. Lift the paper overhang to remove from the pan. Transfer to a flat surface and cut into 8 bars.

5. Serve immediately or store in an airtight container in the refrigerator for up to 2 weeks.

Makes 8 servings.

CANTO "BITES"

No one can deny the decadence of Canto Bight on the planet of Cantonica. The same is true of these jam-filled, bite-size coffee cakes!

INGREDIENTS

2¼	cups (315 grams) all-purpose flour
½	teaspoon salt for seasoning
2	teaspoons ground cinnamon
1	cup (200 grams) packed dark brown sugar
¾	cup (150 grams) granulated sugar
¾	cup (180 millilitres) vegetable oil
1	teaspoon baking powder
1	teaspoon baking soda
1	egg, lightly beaten
1	cup (240 grams) low-fat sour cream
¾	cup (225 grams) raspberry jam
1	cup (120 grams) chopped pecans

1. Preheat the oven to 350°F (180°C).

2. Whisk together the flour, salt, 1 teaspoon of the cinnamon, both sugars, and the oil in a large bowl.

3. Using a large spoon and a measuring cup, scoop out ¾ cup (150 grams) of the mixture and place it in a small bowl. Set aside.

4. Add the baking powder, baking soda, egg, and sour cream to the mixture in the large bowl and stir until just combined. The texture will be slightly lumpy.

5. Line a 12-cup muffin pan with paper liners. Fill each cup halfway with the muffin batter.

6. Carefully spoon about 2 teaspoons of the raspberry jam into the center of the batter in each muffin cup.

7. Top off each muffin cup with the remaining batter.

8. Stir the pecans and the remaining 1 teaspoon cinnamon into the flour mixture in the small bowl. Sprinkle it evenly over the tops of the muffin cups.

9. Bake until a wooden skewer inserted into the center of a cake comes out clean, 15 to 20 minutes.

10. Cool the cakes in the pan on a wire rack for 10 minutes. Remove the cakes from the pan and place on the wire rack until cooled completely. Store in an airtight container for up to 3 days.

Makes 12 coffee cakes.

REYSIN BREAD

Rey's bread rises instantly when water is added. This bread takes a while longer to rise in the oven, but it's worth the wait!

INGREDIENTS

4	cups (560 grams) plus 1 tablespoon all-purpose flour
¼	cup (50 grams) sugar
1	teaspoon baking soda
1½	teaspoons salt for seasoning
1	tablespoon matcha powder
¼	cup (55 grams) cold butter, cut into 8 pieces
1¾	cups (420 millilitres) low-fat buttermilk
1	egg, lightly beaten
1	cup (140 grams) raisins

1. Preheat the oven to 350°F (180°C).

2. Put 4 cups (560 grams) of the flour, the sugar, baking soda, salt, and matcha powder in the bowl of a standing mixer fitted with a paddle attachment. Mix on low until combined. Add the butter and continue to mix on low until the mixture resembles coarse meal.

3. In a separate medium bowl, whisk together the buttermilk and egg, then pour into the flour-butter mixture. Stir with a wooden spoon until a soft and sticky dough forms.

4. In a small bowl, toss the raisins with the remaining 1 tablespoon flour, then stir them into the dough until they are evenly distributed.

5. Turn the dough out onto a floured work surface. Knead and turn the dough a few times before forming it into a flat, round loaf on an ungreased baking sheet. Using a sharp knife, slash two deep lines across the dough's surface.

6. Bake for 30 to 40 minutes, until lightly browned and the loaf sounds hollow when tapped with your knuckle. Cool for 15 minutes before slicing. Store in an airtight container for up to 3 days.

Makes 1 loaf.

PRETZ-WING FIGHTERS

INGREDIENTS

One	¼-ounce (7 grams) package or 2½ teaspoons active dry yeast
1	teaspoon salt for seasoning
1	tablespoon sugar
1½	cups (360 millilitres) warm water, 105°F–110°F (40°C–43°C)
4	cups (560 grams) plus 1 tablespoon all-purpose flour
1	teaspoon ground cinnamon
½	cup (70 grams) raisins
⅓	cup (40 grams) finely chopped walnuts
1	egg, beaten

1. Preheat the oven to 425°F (220°C). Butter a baking sheet.

2. In a small bowl, sprinkle the yeast, salt, and sugar over the warm water and set aside until bubbly, about 10 minutes.

3. Meanwhile, stir together 4 cups (560 grams) of the flour and the cinnamon in a large bowl. In a small bowl, toss the raisins and walnuts with the remaining 1 tablespoon flour, then stir them into the flour mixture.

4. Add the yeast mixture to the flour mixture and stir to combine.

5. Turn the dough out onto a floured work surface and knead until smooth and elastic, 5 to 7 minutes.

6. Divide the dough into 12 pieces. Using your hands, roll each piece into a 12-inch (30.5-centimetre) rope.

7. Cut each rope in half and press the halves together to form an X, then place the X-shaped pretzels onto the prepared baking sheet.

8. Using a pastry brush, brush the pretzel dough with the beaten egg.

9. Bake the pretzels until golden brown, 12 to 15 minutes. Cool for 10 minutes before serving.

Makes 12 pretzels.

SANDWICHES & WRAPS

Breakfast Poe'Boy
Kanjiklub Sandwiches
Breakfast Tako-danas

BREAKFAST POE'BOY

Poe Dameron is the best pilot in the Resistance. You won't be able to resist this delicious layered breakfast sandwich.

INGREDIENTS

4	teaspoons butter
¼	cup (30 grams) chopped red or green bell pepper
¼	cup (35 grams) chopped onion
3	eggs
¼	cup (35 grams) chopped ham
1	French or whole wheat roll, sliced in half

1. In a skillet over medium heat, melt 2 teaspoons of the butter. Add the bell pepper and onion and cook, stirring frequently, until the onion is translucent, 2 to 3 minutes. Using tongs or a large spoon, transfer the vegetables to a plate and set aside.

2. Return the skillet to medium heat. Crack the eggs into a small bowl and whisk with a fork to combine. Pour the eggs into the skillet and swirl to distribute them evenly. Cook until the edges of the eggs are dry. Add the vegetables and ham to the center of the omelette and cook until the eggs are set, about 1 to 2 minutes. Using a spatula, fold the sides of the omelette over the filling. Remove the skillet from the heat.

3. Toast the roll and butter the cut sides with the remaining 2 teaspoons butter. Place the omelette on the bottom of the roll and cover with the top. Cut in half and serve immediately.

Makes 2 servings.

KANJIKLUB SANDWICHES

Kanjiklub demands the debt that Han Solo owes them. When you're ravenous as a rathtar, you'll demand to have this delicious sandwich for breakfast!

INGREDIENTS

3	slices sourdough or whole wheat bread
2	tablespoons cream cheese, at room temperature
2	eggs
1	teaspoon butter
	Salt and pepper for seasoning
4	bacon slices, cooked
2	large slices tomato
1	romaine lettuce leaf

1. Lightly toast the bread in a toaster or toaster oven.

2. Spread the cream cheese evenly on the top of each slice.

3. Crack the eggs into a small bowl.

4. Heat a nonstick skillet over medium heat, add the butter, and swirl until it melts and coats the skillet.

5. Gently pour the eggs into the skillet and tilt the skillet slightly to one side to pool all of the eggs together. As the egg white begins to turn opaque, set the skillet back down.

6. Season the eggs with salt and pepper and cook for 1 to 2 minutes, until the yolks begin to set but remain slightly jiggly. Flip the eggs over with a spatula and cook until the yolks are set, 1 to 2 minutes more.

7. Remove the cooked eggs from the skillet with a spatula and place on one of the prepared slices of bread. Top the egg with another slice of bread, cream cheese–side up. Add the bacon, tomato, and lettuce. Then top with the third slice of bread, cream cheese–side down.

8. Slice in half and serve immediately.

Makes 2 servings.

BREAKFAST TAKO-DANAS

After a life spent on the dry, desert planet of Jakku, Rey is shocked when she lands on the beautiful green planet of Takodana. Inspired by the lush planet, these tangy tacos have a beautiful green filling.

INGREDIENTS

Four	6-inch (15-centimetre) corn tortillas
2	teaspoons olive oil
7	cups (140 grams) stemmed and washed spinach leaves
	Salt and pepper
1/4	cup (55 grams) green tomatillo salsa
4	eggs, beaten
1/2	cup (40 grams) shredded low-fat Monterey Jack cheese

1. Preheat the oven to 350°F (180°C).

2. Wrap the tortillas in aluminum foil and place on an ungreased baking sheet or directly on the oven rack. Heat for 10 minutes while you prepare the filling.

3. Heat the olive oil in a 12-inch (30.5-centimetre) nonstick skillet over medium heat. Add the spinach and sauté until wilted, 3 to 5 minutes. Season with salt and pepper, then use tongs to remove the spinach from the skillet and place on a plate.

4. Remove the skillet from the heat and, using the tongs, wipe out the skillet with a paper towel.

5. Coat the skillet with nonstick cooking spray.

6. Return the skillet to medium heat, add the salsa, and cook for 2 to 3 minutes to evaporate the extra water.

7. Pour the beaten eggs into the skillet.

Continued

8. When the edges start to set, use a wooden spoon or spatula to gently push the eggs to the center and tilt the skillet to distribute the uncooked eggs. Swirl the eggs to distribute the uncooked eggs to the surface of the skillet. Continue scraping until the eggs are just cooked through, about 2 minutes. They will be fluffy and appear just a little wet, but not liquidy.

9. Add the cooked spinach and cook, stirring continuously, until the mixture is completely heated through, 1 to 2 minutes.

10. Remove the warmed tortillas from the foil and fill each one with one-quarter of the egg mixture and 2 tablespoons of the cheese. Serve immediately.

Makes 4 servings.

SPREADS & TOPPINGS

A Tight Jam
"Light It Up" Lemon Curd

A TIGHT JAM

Rose and Finn are in a tight jam in Canto Bight.
You'll free your tastebuds when savoring this jam
on toast or pancakes.

INGREDIENTS

2	cups (280 grams) fresh strawberries, hulled and sliced
2	tablespoons sugar
1	tablespoon fresh lemon juice

Special equipment: 1 lidded pint jar, washed in hot, soapy water and rinsed thoroughly

1. Place a small ceramic plate in the refrigerator to chill.

2. Combine the strawberries, sugar, and lemon juice in a saucepan and cook over medium heat, stirring constantly and mashing with a wooden spoon.

3. When the mixture comes to a boil, turn the heat to low and simmer for 10 minutes, stirring frequently.

4. Test the jam for doneness by using a wooden spoon to drop a small amount onto the chilled plate and then swirling it around. If the jam is sticky, it's ready. If the jam is runny, cook it for 5 minutes more and test again.

5. Using a ladle, carefully transfer the jam to the pint jar to cool. When the jam has cooled, cover and store in the refrigerator for up to 1 week.

Makes approximately 1½ cups (450 grams).

"LIGHT IT UP" LEMON CURD

This sprightly spread will add a bright flavor to muffins, toast, pancakes, or waffles.

INGREDIENTS

5	**egg yolks**
½	**cup (100 grams) sugar**
¼	**cup (60 millilitres) fresh lemon juice**
	Zest of 1 lemon
6	**tablespoons (90 grams) butter, cut into 6 pieces**

1. Stir together the egg yolks, sugar, lemon juice, and lemon zest in a saucepan. Cook over medium heat, stirring constantly, until the mixture thickens and bubbles begin to form, 6 to 7 minutes. Remove from the heat and add the butter, 1 tablespoon at time, stirring until melted after each addition.

2. Transfer to a glass bowl, then lightly press plastic wrap onto the surface of the lemon curd. Refrigerate for 2 hours or overnight.

3. Serve as a topping for toast, biscuits, pancakes, or waffles. Serve immediately or store covered in the refrigerator for up to 2 weeks.

Makes about 1¼ cups (300 millilitres).

Vitamin C-3PO
Jakku Juice

VITAMIN C-3PO

This fruity smoothie will revive you as your day begins!

INGREDIENTS

1	cup (240 grams) low-fat vanilla Greek yogurt
1	cup (240 millilitres) apple juice
1	cup (240 millilitres) low-fat milk
2	tablespoons honey
1	large banana, sliced
12	large strawberries, sliced, plus 2 whole strawberries

1. Put the yogurt, apple juice, milk, honey, banana, and sliced strawberries into a blender and process on medium speed until well combined. Pour into two tall glasses.

2. Using a knife, cut a slit in each of the whole strawberries, from the bottom halfway up toward the stem. Position a strawberry on the rim of each glass as a garnish. Serve immediately.

Makes 2 servings.

JAKKU JUICE

It's hot and dry on Rey's home planet, Jakku. Quench your thirst with this bright and energizing drink.

INGREDIENTS

4	**orange wedges**
1	**cup (240 millilitres) pineapple juice**
1	**cup (240 millilitres) fresh orange juice**
1	**cup (240 millilitres) sparkling water**
½	**teaspoon peeled grated fresh ginger**

1. The night before serving, cut each orange wedge in half crosswise and place each half wedge into a compartment of an ice cube tray. Top off the compartments with the pineapple juice and freeze overnight.

2. The next day, make the sparklers: Fill each of two tall glasses with ½ cup (120 millilitres) of the orange juice and ½ cup (120 millilitres) of the sparkling water. Add ¼ teaspoon of the ginger to each and stir to combine. Add 4 juice ice cubes to each glass. Serve immediately.

Makes 2 servings.